Taking the
LIMITS
off
GOD

Taking the
LIMITS
off
GOD

Dr. James B. Richards

rill &
associates

Taking the Limits Off God

ISBN: 978-0-9832536-2-4

Printed in the United States of America.

©1989 by James B. Richards

Rill and Associates
P.O. Box 119
Orrstown, PA 17244

303.503.7257

www.rillandassociates.com

First Printing, January 1989
Second Printing, June 1990
Third Printing, March 1997
Fourth Printing, April 2011

1 2 3 4 5 6 7 8 9 10 / 15 14 13 12 11

Table of Contents

Introduction

When I gave my life to the Lord, I sold out to Him totally. I had a supernatural encounter with God and my commitment to Him was absolute. I had seen too much of the "nonsense of religion" and I knew I did not want to become a carbon copy of the Christians I had known. My prayer of commitment to the Lord went like this: "Get me to a Bible. I'll read it, believe it, and do what it says, but I will never *play church*." I wanted to know the God of the Bible, not the God of man's imagination.

Although I started out with a supernatural walk with the Lord, eventually, I found myself in the very trap I had wanted to avoid: I was limiting God by seeing Him, not as He really is, but as I had been taught that He is.

The twentieth century church is a product of years of unbelief, handed down from generation to generation. Like the Pharisees of

Jesus' day, our doctrines are "the traditions and the commandments of men." We have limited God to the unbelief of our predecessors. That is the reason the church today is not seeing the power of God manifested in signs and wonders and mighty miracles.

Like the prophet Elisha, we must boldly ask, "Where is the God of Elijah?" If we are not seeing miracles in our day, we must acknowledge that God has not changed (James 1:17); we are the ones who have limited what He can do in our day. God is willing to be everything to us that He was to any person named in the Bible. The only thing that has changed is our perception of God.

Each chapter in this book is designed to be short enough to be read in one sitting. Each is a self-contained lesson about the ways we have been taught to limit God and how we can stop doing so. Pause after you read each chapter and ask the Lord to show you how you have been limiting Him. Ask Him to remove any limits you have placed on what He can do in your life.

Chapter 1

Lost in
the Wilderness

We are all familiar with the story of Moses and the children of Israel. After Moses led the Israelites out of slavery in Egypt, they spent forty, very difficult years wandering in the desert before they could enter the promised land. The Bible presents us with a detailed picture of this period of trial and testing that has become known as "the wilderness experience."

While most Christians today will probably never get lost in a literal desert, many of us have struggled with chronic physical illness, financial problems, or bondage to some besetting sin. You may know what it means to lose sight of your heart's desire. Your goal, your *promised land*, can seem just as unreachable as Canaan land must have seemed to the children of Israel.

Like the children of Israel, we have escaped from slavery. When we accepted Jesus, we were set free from bondage to sin and to our old nature. But, like the children of Israel, many of us seem incapable of living the abundant life. It is one thing to be set free from slavery; it is quite another thing to be free enough from our former way of thinking to be able to enter the promised land! Like the children of Israel before us, we often choose to live in the wilderness because we do not believe God is able to lead us into the promised land.

Psalm 78:41 gives us some insight into the wilderness mentality: *"Yea, they turned back and tempted God."* They refused to believe the promise was for them. They did not believe God was really able to give them the abundant life. Since they did not believe the promise, they were unable to receive it. The Psalmist goes on to say, *"THEY LIMITED THE HOLY ONE OF ISRAEL."*

When the Bible says they "tempted God," it means they put God on trial. Instead of believing His promises and testing His Word to see if it would work, they put Him on trial as if in a court of law. They did not believe God was able to perform His promises. They tried Him and found Him guilty of lying. Since they did not believe God's promises, they did not obey His Word. As a result, they found themselves wandering in the wilderness.

The children of Israel saw great miracles performed on their behalf in the land of Egypt. They witnessed the plagues against the Egyptians. They saw the Red Sea part. They ate the manna from heaven every day. They had an intellectual understanding that God could do anything, yet when they saw the size of the enemy in the land of Canaan (there were giants in the land!), they were unable to believe that God could give them victory over their circumstances.

Like the children of Israel, we turn our backs on God and limit the Holy One of Israel. *"For unto us was the Gospel preached, as well as unto them: but the Word preached did not profit them, not being mixed with faith in them that heard it."* Hebrews 4:2. Like the Israelites, we look at the size of the enemy holding our inheritance and we feel inadequate in our own eyes (Numbers 13:33). We limit God in the same way the children of Israel did. We say, "Oh, I know God *can* do anything." But we are not convinced that He *will* do it in our lives and in our circumstances.

It is possible to be saved, called, and chosen of God, yet like the children of Israel, to live and die without ever entering into your promised inheritance. It is possible for your entire Christian walk to be one of wondering and wavering, trials and temptations, never knowing exactly where you are or where you are going.

Yet Jesus came to set us free from these things. So why is it so difficult for us to lay hold of that freedom? I believe it is because we have been taught to put unbiblical restrictions on God in such areas as healing, prosperity, deliverance, and living in victory. There are many today who actually believe that the *wilderness experience* is a normal part of the Christian life. Some have even come to embrace it as necessary for Christian growth. Because of unscriptural, mystical thinking, we feel the wilderness is somehow ordained of God. We limit what God can do in our lives.

Did God design the *wilderness experience* to purify His people? I don't think so. When God called the children of Israel out of the land of Egypt, it was not His plan to make them wander in the wilderness for forty years. He intended for that generation of His people to immediately receive their promised inheritance. And yet, that whole generation died without ever seeing it. What went wrong?

The reason that generation of the children of Israel did not receive the promise is found plainly in Hebrews 3.19: *"So we see that they could not enter in because of unbelief."* Hebrews 11:6 says, *"Without faith, it is impossible to please God."* This Bible kind of faith believes that *". . . He is the rewarder of them that diligently seek Him."* Hebrew 11:6. They did not believe God would keep His Word and it was their unbelief, not God's desire to purify them, that kept them out of the promised land!

Hebrews 11:13 says that the men and women of faith *". . .saw the promises afar off."* That is exactly how many Christians today see the promises — afar off. They acknowledge that the promises are true, but they see them as meant for the distant future. The writer of Hebrews warned the church about the need to enter into the promises of God (Hebrews 4:1). *"There remaineth a rest to the people of God . . . Let us labor therefore to enter into that rest."* Hebrews 4:9,11. We should desire to enter into the abundant life, not out of a motivation of greed, but because it is a Bible mandate. We are commanded to enter in.

Moses realized that if the children of Israel did not enter the land as God had promised them, surrounding heathen nations would say that God did not keep His Word or that He was unable to deliver His people. In the same way, the world today looks at a church that is failing to enter into the abundant life, and smugly concludes that faith does not work or God is not able.

The writer of the book of Hebrews sternly warns us, *"Let us therefore FEAR, lest, a promise being left us of entering into his rest, any of you should seem to come short of it."* Hebrews 4:1. The rest spoken of in the Old Testament was the land of Canaan, flowing with milk and honey, but this rest was only a type of the rest God has for the New Testament believer. Our rest is the abundant life, which Jesus promised us (John 10:10).

This New Testament "rest" is more than salvation. The children of Israel had already been "saved" from slavery in Egypt. When we accept Christ, we are saved from slavery to sin. Our goal now must be to enter into our inheritance: the promised land of abundant life, which Jesus died to give us.

Chapter 2

The Destructive Power of Negative Thinking

Why is it so hard for us to take the Bible at face value in the areas of healing, prosperity, and deliverance? Why do we have so much trouble accepting that the promises in the Bible are for us? Why have we lost the ability to accept the plain sense of the Word of God?

The answer, in a word, is negativism. We are programmed from childhood to think negatively, to expect bad instead of good. As a result, we limit ourselves and what we can accomplish in life. Most of us dream of things we would like to achieve, but only a tiny percentage actually succeed in fulfilling even a small part of our life's dream. How easy it is to fall into the trap of confessing the Word with our mouths, but wavering in our hearts. Negativism attacks and ultimately destroys our faith and hope, until our dreams are abandoned in an atmosphere of frustration and despair.

Hope is an essential element of faith. I do not mean the kind of hope that says "Someday God might do something for me." The word translated *hope* in the New Testament means "confident expectation (of good)." Bible hope is the breeding ground of faith. Without a confident expectation of good, we will never be able to work real faith.

Once hope (the confident expectation of good) is destroyed, fear takes over. Fear is the opposite of Bible hope: it confidently expects the worst. Fear is the breeding ground for unbelief, which always leads to disobedience. This process of fear and unbelief starts in childhood, and often lasts a lifetime. Once the simple faith of early childhood is lost, it is not easily regained.

Jesus told us that we must become as little children (Matthew 18:3). Young children possess a quality that is essential to achieving their dreams: they know no limits! They do not know what they can't do, so they dream big dreams. They are limited only by their imaginations. But, indoctrination into negative thinking begins all too early.

Research has shown[1] that few adults can be classified as highly creative, whereas 95% of all four-year-olds are highly creative.

---

1. Brian Tracey, Psychology of Achievement (Nightingale-Conant Co.).

The truly astonishing aspect of this research is that while 95% of all four-year-olds studied were considered creative, only 4% of all seven-year-olds studied retain their creativity. What happened to these children in the three years between four and seven? The answer is obvious: they started school.

Pre-school children are expected to be imaginative. However, when children start school, they enter what we call the "real world." The real world is intolerant of dreamers. In school, away from the nurturing of our parents, we begin to learn all the things we *cannot* do. We are compared unfavorably to others. We are stereotyped. We are encouraged to abandon our own ideas in favor of conformity to a group standard. We are discouraged from developing our imaginations. Our hopes and dreams fall victim to negative input from teachers and peers. We sacrifice our individuality on the altar of peer pressure.

From childhood, our thoughts are programmed for what we *cannot* do rather than for what we *can* do. Our self-image is so fragile that we cannot bear the possibility of failure, so we limit what we are willing to try. When we get saved and begin developing a new relationship with God, we continue to limit ourselves with the negativism of our former selves. In so doing, we limit God as well. We are inclined to doubt the promises of God because they do not square with our limited self concepts.

The only limitations that God has are those in your mind! When we get saved, we are told to renew our minds so that we may know what is the good and acceptable and perfect will of God (Romans 12:2). Many new Christians think the battle they fight is with their old nature, so they are always trying to crucify their flesh.

Your old nature is already crucified with Jesus (Romans 6:6 and Galatians 2:20). There is nothing that can be added to what is already done. *"You are not in the flesh, but in the Spirit, if it so be that the Spirit of God dwell in you. Now if any man have not the Spirit of Christ, he is none of His."* Romans 8:9.

Your problem is not your old nature; it is your old way of thinking. Before you got saved, you were programmed to a way of thinking and handling problems. You had your own ideas about what was good and bad, right and wrong, and what your abilities and limitations were.

When you received Jesus, you became a new creation. All the old has gone, and the new has come (2 Corinthians 5:17). In order to live this new life to the fullest of your potential, you must renew your thinking. You must accept God's standards of right and wrong, good and bad, and what you are able to accomplish. Otherwise, you will always limit what God can do in your life by your negative thinking.

Jay Adams says, in his book *The Christian Counselors Manual,*[2] that it only takes 3–6 weeks to develop a habit. A godly habit can be developed in the same length of time it takes to develop an ungodly habit. If we can develop the ability to believe God's Word, to see God's answer instead of focusing on the problem, we can remove all the limitations that we have placed on God.

The Bible exhorts us to *". . . exercise yourselves unto godliness."* 1 Timothy 4:7. We have to **practice** being godly! That means you

2. Jay E. Adams, The Christian Counselors Manual (Grand Rapids, MI: Baker Book House, 1973).

work at it: you do it, and do it, and do it, until it becomes a habit. If we practice taking control over our thoughts, rejecting negativism, and nurturing positive faith thinking, in six weeks we will have laid the foundation to change the course of our entire lives. Six weeks is a small investment to make for so great a return!

Chapter 3

Seeing With the Eye of Faith

God has commanded us to meditate on His Word. One definition of the word *meditate* is "to ponder." We are to ponder, or think through, the Word of God. When we meditate, we are using the power of the imagination: our God-given ability to dream.

In Joshua 1:8, God commanded Joshua to meditate. He had to remind himself of God's promises to the nation of Israel. Joshua was able to gain victory over the giants through the power of a mind that was stayed on God's Word (Isaiah 26:3).

Hebrews 11 says that the men and women of faith *"saw the promises afar off and were persuaded of them."* The men of God in the Old Testament spent time meditating on the promises of God. Abraham, Moses, and all those listed in the *roll call of faith* were looking for something that could not be seen with the natural eye. All these great men and women of faith were dreamers.

The Bible tells of many instances in which God spoke to people through dreams. He has also used the sand, the stars, torn garments, broken arrows, and even striped sticks to get people to visualize and think about His Word. He used these things to help us see the unseen.

Acts 2:17 says that the Holy Spirit will cause us to dream dreams. Dreams are thoughts dwelt upon, whether we are awake or asleep. If we would allow God to stimulate our ability to dream so that we could see His promises as real, we would be immovable in the face of trouble.

The Apostle Paul says that, prior to salvation, we were alienated from God through the darkness of our minds (Colossians 1:21). Our wicked imaginations were continually evil because our imaginative powers were perverted by the sinful nature.

However, when we submit ourselves to the Lordship of Jesus, sin no longer has dominion over us (Romans 6:14). God commands us to be renewed in the spirit of our mind (Ephesians 4:23). We can then recover our imaginative abilities and develop them for the glory of God. We are free to yield to righteousness what was previously yielded to unrighteousness (Romans 6:13). As we renew our minds (Romans 12:2), we can begin to use our imaginations as God intended, to see ourselves as great men and women of God, to aspire to greatness for God.

All the deeds of men, both good and evil, were first conceived in the imagination. (If you can conceive it and believe it, you can achieve it.) Many of us have learned to fear developing our imaginative powers, our ability to dream, but there is no scriptural reason to consider the imagination itself to be evil. While the imagination has often been put to evil use, the Bible makes it clear that our imaginative power is a gift from God, meant for good, not evil.

Romans 4:17 says that God Himself calls those things that are not as though they were. Paul said *". . . We look not at the things which are seen, but at the things which are not seen: for the things which are seen are temporal; but the things which are not seen are eternal."* 2 Corinthians 4:18. Paul looked at the invisible. He developed the ability to see things that cannot be seen by the natural eye. He was even accused of being crazy because of his faith in the unseen (Acts 26:24). But a dreamer has the ability to see the intangible.

How did Paul see the invisible? In 2 Corinthians 5:7 he says, *"We walk by faith and not by sight."* Paul could see the invisible with the eye of faith. People only believe what they can see, and there are only two ways to see: with the natural eye, and with the eye of faith.

The eye of faith sees with the heart. Strong's Concordance defines the word *heart* as the mind. Faith is a matter of what is conceived in the mind (heart) through the Word of God. As we read God's Word, we yield to His Spirit and incubate the promises that God has given us in His Word.

Doing this effectively involves using our imaginations. We must meditate on those promises that seem so far away. Meditating on God's Word gives the Holy Spirit the opportunity to persuade us that the promises are true, and that they are for us, here and now. Until we, too, can see the unseen promises of God, we will limit God to our own experience.

Chapter 4

The Importance of Self-Esteem

Jesus said we must become as little children to enter the kingdom of heaven (Matthew 18:3). Before entering school, a child's sense of self-worth is derived from the love and acceptance shown by his parents. Consistent parental love (in spite of early childhood failures) is essential for the formation of a healthy sense of self-worth.

When a young child is learning to walk, he faces one *failure* after another. Day after day, he gets up, falls down, gets up, falls down. He hurts himself occasionally, but he keeps on trying. He *fails* because he is learning a new skill, and mastery of that new skill takes time and practice.

When the toddler falls down, his parents do not tell him he is stupid and clumsy. They pick him up, cuddle him, and encourage him to keep trying. The toddler does not base his sense of self-worth on how soon he masters walking, or on how often he falls before he learns. He bases it on the love and acceptance of his parents.

As adults, most of us derive our self-esteem, not from the love and acceptance of our heavenly Father, but from our ability to succeed at certain tasks. We feel good about ourselves based on our accomplishments, rather than on who we are in Jesus. This can be compared to *righteousness by works*. We try to *earn* our self-esteem.

This way of thinking begins in school, when a child no longer receives the unconditional love and acceptance he had at home. His self-image comes from comparing himself to his classmates. Out of a fear of ridicule if he fails, or perhaps out of a fear of being different, he begins to limit the things he is willing to try.

Consider the child who plays baseball for the first time. The game appears simple enough. He watched the older boys hit home runs and he believes he can hit them, too. But the first pitch goes by so fast. He swings and misses. The second pitch is another strike. The older kids ridicule him and his enthusiasm and confidence begin to wane. Strike three. The little fellow gives up and goes home feeling rejected and discouraged. He will be hesitant to join the baseball game next time, out of fear of ridicule. This hesitancy and fear further wound his self-esteem.

Or consider the six-year-old who announces to his mother, "When I grow up, I'm going to be president!" His well-meaning mother does not want her son to experience disappointment, so she discourages him from setting such unrealistic goals. She tells him the reasons why he will not grow up to be president. His confidence and self-image both take a nose dive. His own mother does not believe in him or in his dream. Next time, he will not dream so big or aim so high. As he gets older, he will get used to people telling him what he cannot do, and the scope of his vision will become increasingly narrow. (Somewhere in the world, a wise mother is saying, "Son, you can grow up to be anything you want to be!" After all, every president was once a six-year-old with a dream.)

Trying to protect our children from disappointment, we teach them to curb their expectations, thereby limiting their potential. Disappointment is a part of life. Sheltering a child from disappointment will make him afraid to launch out as an adult. By surviving the disappointments of childhood, a child learns the necessary art of overcoming setbacks. When parents overprotect a child, they deny his ability to succeed. The child comes to see himself as a failure, which leads to the deepest form of self-rejection. We must realize that every opportunity for success also presents a risk of failure. Trying to protect a child from risk automatically denies him the opportunity to be successful.

God is a loving Father, and like any loving father, He understands that His children will fall occasionally as they learn to walk in faith. If you try and fail, God still loves you and accepts you, but if you draw back, He has no pleasure in you. (Hebrews 10:38).

As you learn to walk by faith, you please your heavenly Father. The man of faith may fall, but he never quits. He knows that even when he falls, his heavenly Father still loves and accepts him. *"Though he fall, he shall not be utterly cast down: for the Lord upholdeth him with His hand."* Psalm 37:24. Like the toddler learning to walk, his self-worth is derived from the loving relationship he has with his Father through the Lord Jesus, and not from his achievements (works). God's love for us does not fluctuate with our successes and defeats. Ephesians 1:6 says, *"He has made us accepted in the beloved* [Jesus]. *"*

Childhood incidents can forever affect a person's willingness to try new things or to dream big dreams. It is not so much the fear of failure, as it is the fear of looking or sounding ridiculous to others. As a child, I had a terrible self-image. I was ashamed to talk in public. In school, I would often refuse to answer the teacher when she called on me, because I was afraid of sounding foolish. I was often paddled for my lack of cooperation, but paddling was better than *looking dumb.*

How often we limit what we will allow God to do in our lives for fear of looking foolish if it does not happen! Intelligent people read God's promises in the Bible every day, but continue in sickness and disease because they are afraid to believe His Word, afraid to fail if they launch out in faith. Many people would rather die of cancer than risk looking foolish by believing what the Bible says about healing.

The concepts of self-esteem, self-image, and self-worth have a great deal to do with the limitations we place upon ourselves. These concepts largely determine our future successes and failures. Preserving the self-worth is a powerful motivation to action, while fear of failure and its effects on the self-image is an equally powerful inhibitor. Some people will suffer much and even die to avoid losing face, while others will try to avoid situations in which failure and loss-of-face are possibilities.

A person who ventures out to explore the unknown (to boldly go where no man has gone before) does so partly to increase his self-esteem. Another man can look at the same venture and refuse to chance it for fear of losing self-esteem. In both cases, self-esteem is powerful as a motivator or de-motivator. On the one hand, it can spur a man on to action; on the other hand, it can render another man powerless in the face of the same challenge.

Nothing succeeds like success, but failure breeds fear of more failure. Jesus put it this way, *"Unto everyone that hath shall be given, and he shall have abundance: but from him that hath not shall be taken away even that which he hath."* Matthew 25:29.

Chapter 5

Circumstance Theology

When an organization loses its original vision, it stops growing. It loses the excitement and fervor that marked its early days. It enters the *justification stage*, where its energies are spent trying to justify its existence rather than achieving its original goals.

When the early church stopped doing what Jesus said to do, it began to grow cold and powerless. Signs and wonders no longer occurred because the Word was not taught. This lack of power forced the church into the justification stage. Instead of repenting and turning back to God, they began to invent new doctrine consistent with their experience. This new doctrine enabled them to preserve their self-esteem. I call this *circumstance theology*.

a theology based on circumstances or personal experience rather than on what the Bible says.

The modern church is a product of years of adhering to circumstance theology, thereby limiting what God can do in our day. Today, if a Christian actually believes what Jesus had to say about healing or prosperity, he is branded an extremist or even a heretic.

When I preach on one of God's great promises, such as prosperity, I give dozens of scriptures to support the promise. I go overboard to point out that the main reason God wants us to be prosperous is to give us the resources to reach the world for Jesus. (This should be our motivation also, rather than merely desiring prosperity to line our own pockets.)

After the service, invariably, someone will approach me and complain about the message. "I don't believe that prosperity message," they say. I ask them, "Why don't you believe it?" The answer is always the same: "Because it doesn't work for me." But if God's Word says it, *"Let God be true and every man a liar."* Romans 3:4. If it is not working in your life, it is because you are limiting God. For most of us, it is easier to blame God than to admit that we are to blame for limiting what God can do in our lives. As God asked Job, *"Wilt thou condemn Me, that thou mayest be righteous?"* Job 40:8.

We, like Job, have such a fragile sense of self-worth that we would rather blame God than admit we are wrong. It is time for the church to realize that if God's promises are not working in our lives, it is not because the promises have changed in our day. It is not because God has changed; it is because we have changed. We are no longer alive with faith as the early Christians were.

A minister who watched me cast a homosexual spirit out of a young boy said to me, "I know that's in the Bible, and I just watched you do it, but I don't believe in casting out demons." He probably did not realize it, but he was basically saying, "I'll deny God's integrity before I will allow my self-image to be threatened."

Acting in unbelief and fear, we commit foolishness in our hearts. Then we blame God in order to preserve our self-esteem. Proverbs 19:3 expresses this clearly: *"The foolishness of man perverteth his way: and his heart fretteth against the Lord."* We, as believers, do not usually blame God by attacking Him directly. We blame Him by denying the present reality of His promises.

The need to preserve self-esteem is a key element in how well we operate faith. If you step out in faith and fail, it is not because the Word of God is not true. Any time there is a discrepancy between your experience and the Word of God, the problem is with you, not with the Word.

In Bible terms, what is success and what is failure? Success is persistence in reaching a desired goal, despite how long it takes. Failure is giving up before the goal is reached. The Bible says, *"For though a righteous man falls seven times, he rises again."* Proverbs 24:16 (NIV). It does not say that the righteous never fall. God can see the righteousness of our hearts when we get up again and persist in believing His Word. Remember, Abraham was counted as righteous because he believed, not because he never failed.

It is easy to forget that every great man has had his share of failures on the way to becoming a success. A person only becomes a failure when he quits. The same principle applies when it comes to operating faith. If we give up on working faith because we tried it once and it did not work, we are failures. What is worse, we often blame God for our failures, when we ourselves have limited what He can do in our lives by our own unbelief. We must never interpret the Word of God by our circumstances. We must boldly believe and cling to God's promises whether we are receiving them or not.

Everything Is Possible for Him Who Believes

If we can believe, all things are possible to us! This is not a frivolous statement; it is a promise from God. When we exercise faith, we can receive every promise of God. Belief is the one and only requirement.

Mark 9:14–29 tells the story of a man who brought his son to Jesus to be delivered of a demon. Now, this man must have had a measure of hope that Jesus could heal his son, because he took the trouble to bring his son to Jesus. The disciples tried unsuccessfully to cast the demon out of the boy. No doubt, the unsuccessful efforts of the disciples caused the father's faith to waver even further.

When the demon in the boy saw Jesus, the demon threw the boy on the ground, causing him to foam at the mouth. The demon was making a last ditch effort to destroy what remained of the *father's* faith. Jesus, however, did not make the same mistake the disciples had made. The disciples tried to cast the demon out of the boy without first dealing with the unbelief of the boy's father. I believe Jesus was addressing the boy's father, not the disciples, when He said, *"Oh, unbelieving generation!. . ."* Mark 9:19 (NIV).

The boy had been exhibiting signs of demon possession for years. The father had seen his son hurl himself into fire and water as the demon sought to destroy the boy. The father had to rescue his son from drowning, fighting the demonic power that sought to drive the boy to suicide. Undoubtedly, when the convulsions first began, the father must have prayed earnestly to God to heal his son. However, as time passed and the convulsions continued, the father probably did what many of us do today: he adopted a theology that says that God must have sent the sickness.

But when the father heard that a man from Nazareth was preaching about the kingdom of God, healing the sick, and casting out demons, his hope was revived. However, the father's unbelief had placed limitations on what God could do for his son, and so the first attempt at deliverance was unsuccessful.

The man had come to Jesus because he had heard of the mighty works Jesus did everywhere He went: blind eyes were opened, deaf ears could hear, the mute could speak, withered limbs were made whole, lepers were cleansed, and yes, demons were cast out. This man knew very well that Jesus had done all these things for others, but when it came to *his own situation* he had trouble believing that Jesus could do it for *him, in his circumstance.*

Although the boy was in the midst of a serious convulsion, Jesus first turned to the boy's father. He first had to identify and remove the limitations the father's unbelief had caused. Tension must have filled the air as Jesus calmly questioned the man, while his son writhed on the ground in the midst of a violent convulsion. Out of his despair, the father spoke and his words defined the problem clearly: *"If thou CAN do anything,* have compassion on us, and help us. " Mark 9:22 (emphasis mine).

This father was obviously confused. He thought Jesus had to decide or agree to help in this situation. He knew Jesus could heal, but he was not sure if He would do it this time. Just like many Christians today, He was waiting for God to decide to act on his behalf, while God was waiting for him to get his faith in line with the Word!

Jesus placed the responsibility squarely where it belonged: *"If* You can! Everything is possible *for him who believes."* Jesus was saying to the man, "I *am* willing. But My willingness won't heal your son unless **YOU BELIEVE** that I am able to work in **YOUR** circumstance."

Isn't that a bit like the sick person who attends a healing service thinking, "It can't hurt," but without any real faith that healing works or if it does, not believing it can work for him? He would like to believe in healing or he would not be there, but he is basically a skeptic.

In my crusades, I often see people healed from serious diseases who will probably never live for God. At first, that upset me.

Self-righteousness would rise up in me and say, "These people don't deserve to get healed. I know a lot of good people who ought to be getting healed instead of these people." The only difference between the good people who weren't getting healed and the unregenerate people who were getting healed was in the level of their faith. The ones who got healed certainly placed no hope in their personal righteousness, since they had none; but they did believe that healing was real and that it could work for them. The ones who did not get healed may have wanted healing just as much, but perhaps they felt unworthy. In any case, they doubted whether God would do it for them.

The issue is not, "Is God able?" The issue is, "Will He do it for me?" Religious people will admit that God can do anything, but they don't believe He will do it for them. This is a limitation that they place on God. It comes from their feelings of unworthiness, fear of failure, or any of a host of other negative attitudes.

The Bible says in 1 Corinthians 10:13, *"There hath no temptation taken you but such as is common to man."* In other words, you and your situation are not exceptions to the Word. The devil would like each of us to believe there is something so unique about our particular situation that the promises of God somehow do not apply to us. The devil likes to point out flaws in our lives and then tell us that we cannot claim the promises of God because of them. Many of us arrive at the place of believing that God can fulfill His promises, but in our particular case, He is not willing. This conclusion is totally unscriptural. The Word says that He is no respecter of persons: there are no exceptions (Acts 10:34).

Chapter 7

Help My Unbelief!

When I committed my life to Jesus, I meant business. In my salvation prayer, I told God that I would give Him my life, but (not knowing any better at the time) I placed two conditions on my commitment. I said "God, You can have my life. I'm determined to live for You. But I won't *play church*, and I will only believe what I see in the Bible."

I read the New Testament straight through. When I came across something I was supposed to believe, I got down on my knees and said, "All right, Lord, You said I should believe this. I just want to let You know that I do."

When I needed something, I would pray first, then act on my faith. After I prayed for healing, I got up out of bed. When I asked God for the money to make a trip, I would get in the car and go.

I did what the Bible said I should do, and I expected God to do what He said He would do. He never let me down.

Then I joined a charismatic church. I expected my faith to be built up by being around people who had been in the Lord much longer than I had. Unfortunately, that is not what happened.

I was being taught about healing, miracles, prosperity, and the promises of God by people who were not experiencing these things in their own lives. In order to explain this discrepancy between the Word and their experience, my teachers taught me to put all sorts of limitations on God. I was even told that sometimes God Himself puts sickness on people. My faith was quickly reduced to a lot of talk and no power.

My teachers were godly people and much of what they taught me was good. Yet in certain key areas, such as healing, my faith was slowly and methodically being destroyed by the negative teaching and subtle innuendo which took root in my heart. I was taught to limit God in the area of healing.

When I was 28 years old, this issue of sickness and divine healing took on critical importance in my life. I became deathly ill, which turned out to be the beginning of a four-year battle for my very life. For those four years, I tried to get God to heal me. I waited on God to heal me. I did everything I had been taught, but none of it worked. I talked with many pastors, but none of them could show me what God's absolute will was concerning my healing. I spent thousands of dollars on medical bills, lost countless hours from work, and four years later, I was no better.

I had been preaching the full Gospel message for years. I knew what it was to preach about healing, give an invitation, lay hands on the sick, see *them* get healed, and then go home with sickness in my own body. I was able to believe God for help in some areas of my life. I found it easy to believe that God would heal others, but I couldn't believe for my own healing. I, too, had put limitations on God.

Then one morning, I was confessing 2 Corinthians 3:18, the promise of being changed into His image from glory to glory. As I prayed, the Lord spoke to my heart and said, "You are not being changed into My glory. You are being changed into what you have been *told* that I am. You have a religious veil over your heart. You don't see Me as the Healer that I am. You see Me as the kind of healer you were taught that I am."

These words cut me to the quick, but I knew they were true. I had become like the people of Jesus' day. I had traded the life of God for the traditions of men. Jesus said ". . . *Your teachings are but rules taught by men. You have let go of the commands of God and are holding onto the traditions of men.*" Mark 7:7–8 (NIV).

I had accepted tradition over the Word of God, and in doing so, I had rendered the Word ineffective in my life. Mark 7:13 (NIV) says, "*Thus you nullify the Word of God by your tradition. . .*" The Lord showed me plainly that the only way I was going to get help was to get rid of these traditions.

I determined to go home and re-read every scripture about healing. As I did so, the Holy Spirit showed me clearly how I had allowed myself to be deceived about healing. My study brought me to Galatians 3:13: "*Christ hath redeemed us from the curse of the law.*" From that verse, I realized I was completely free from the curse of sickness. I realized that the devil had no right to put any sicknesses on me. I then read 2 Corinthians 1:20, which says that all the promises of God are mine because I am in Jesus. The promises were not mine because I was good enough; they were mine because I was in Jesus.

Like the father with the demon-possessed son, the responsibility was on *me* to remove the limitations I had placed on God and receive what He had already freely given to me in Jesus. It was not a question of God's *ability* to heal me, nor was it a question of His *willingness* to heal me. God had already done His part: past tense. It was up to me to do my part: to believe and act on what He had already done. It was then that I stopped trying to get God to heal me, and simply accepted that healing was mine as part of His finished work.

When I decided to believe God for my healing, I was lying in bed. I accepted the truth of Galatians 3:13. I accepted the truth of 2 Corinthians 1:20. As I struggled to get out of bed, my body cried out with pain. Whenever I felt pain, I worshipped God and thanked Him for His promise. With each pain, I said, "Thank You, Jesus, I am healed by Your stripes. I thank You that sickness cannot stay in my body. I am free from the curse of the law. Thank You for purchasing my healing." Then I would rebuke the pain and continue to do what my body said I could not do.

That day, I repented for being sick. I took my stand against sickness. I rejected all of the traditions I had been taught about healing. I corrected my thoughts, my words, and my faith. When I took the limits off of God, I began walking out my healing, and have been walking it out ever since.

I started out my Christian life in the Word. How had I gotten so far off track? In Hebrews 6:12 it says we are to "... *follow those who, by faith and patience, inherit the promises."* Instead, I had been following the teachings of people who were not inheriting the promises, especially in my own area of greatest need: healing.

If you want advice on how to lose weight, you would not go to another overweight person, even though that person may have read everything there was to read on diets and nutrition. If that "head knowledge" has not translated to results in that person's life, they would not have much practical advice to give you. In fact, their frustration at their own failure to lose weight might discourage you and cause you to doubt whether losing weight is even possible. Or perhaps you would begin to wonder if losing weight was God's will for your life! No, if you want to lose weight, you would seek out someone who had successfully lost weight and kept it off, and then do what they did.

People who do not have the baptism in the Holy Spirit are not qualified to teach about tongues or gifts of the Holy Spirit. Likewise, people who are not walking in God's healing power are not qualified to teach about healing. If you want to learn about healing, find someone who got healed and stays healed, and imitate his faith in that area.

In the same way, if you want to learn about operating the gifts of the Spirit, find someone who flows in those gifts. If you want practical instruction in how to get something to work in your life, find someone who has it working in his own life, someone who is receiving by faith and patience, and then do what he does.

You see, the problem is not with God; it is with us. He is *willing* to heal us, but He is not *able* to heal us *unless* we believe.

Even Jesus Himself was limited in His ministry by the unbelief of others: *"He could do there no mighty work...and He marveled because of their unbelief."* Mark 6:5–6. It is not God's will to keep us sick in order to teach us something. God wants us healed and delivered to teach us something. It is the devil who comes to steal, kill, and destroy. It is our unbelief that limits what God is able to do in our lives.

The father of the demon-possessed boy in Mark 9:24 made a decision. He decided that despite what the religious leaders said, regardless of the many times he had prayed for his son without success, this time he would remove the limitations he had placed on God. He said, "Lord, I believe. Help my unbelief."

He got honest with the Master. He admitted his own complicity in his son's condition: his unbelief. He acknowledged that the root of his son's problem had been his own limited thinking. In a matter of moments, his son was delivered. Why? Because his father had, at last, taken the limits off of God.

Chapter 8

Removing Unbiblical Stipulations

Matthew chapter 9 tells us the story of the woman who had been hemorrhaging for years. She heard about Jesus healing the sick and working mighty miracles. She knew that Jesus had power to heal, but she didn't know what requirements she would have to meet to *qualify* for healing. Historians tell us that there was a superstition in that day regarding touching the hem of the garments. The woman took her faith, such as it was, and mixed it with some local superstition to develop the conditions under which she could believe for healing.

Fortunately, the woman was able to press through the crowd, touch Jesus, and get healed. But you see, she had put conditions on her own faith, as well as on Jesus. Jesus told her, *"Your faith has made you whole."* Matthew 9:22. It wasn't the touching of His garment that healed her; it was her faith. But her ability to operate her faith for healing was contingent on her belief that it was necessary for her to touch the hem of His garment in order for her to be healed. Had she not gotten close enough to Jesus to touch His garment, her faith would not have gone into operation, and she would not have been healed: not because Jesus wasn't willing and able to heal her, but because of the conditions she herself had placed on Jesus for her healing.

How many times do we do likewise? We establish where and under what circumstances we will receive from God. If that situation happens to arise as we imagined it, our faith goes into operation, and sure enough, we get healed. Then we assume that it was our pre-determined set of conditions that allowed us to receive from God. This kind of thinking actually nurtures superstition rather than faith.

Matthew 14:34–36 tells us that an unbiblical doctrine was established as a result of this woman's healing. Word spread that touching the hem of Jesus' garment could heal people, and people began to think that it was necessary for them to touch the hem of His garment in order to be healed.

Matthew 14:36 says, *"And as many as touched were made perfectly whole."* What happened to those who believed that if they could only touch His garment they would be healed, but they weren't able to get close enough to do so? They did not get healed. Not because Jesus wasn't willing, but because their faith had become limited by the unbiblical condition that touching His garment was a necessary prerequisite for healing.

I have heard many great preachers say that few people got healed in their healing lines until the "church people" got out of the way. I wondered what they meant by that, but gradually, I began to understand. Church people who have been taught to place unbiblical limitations on God limit their own faith. They limit what they are able to receive from God based on how they feel. Often un-churched people can hear the simple faith message for the first time, believe, and receive, because their faith has not been damaged or destroyed by wrong teaching.

For many believers, healing, deliverance, and prosperity have been made to sound so complicated, that they feel ignorant and unworthy to receive from God. They have been told to look inside for the reason when they get sick or have financial problems. "Find out what you did to open the door to the devil." This kind of thinking plays right into the devil's hands. He is the accuser of the brethren. When we begin to look for fault in our lives, he helps us find it. Then he tells us we deserve to be sick, broke, or in bondage.

Under the law, failure resulted in the curses, while good behavior brought the blessings. Galatians 3:13 says that Jesus became the curse for us. He took on the curse in our place so we wouldn't have to take it. Since Jesus took the curse in our place, the devil has no authority to try to put it back on us. Jesus set us free from that system once and for all.

New Testament Christians often look back at the old covenant and see the conditions spelled out there for receiving the promises of God. They try to apply these conditions to their own lives. But Galatians 3:13 tells us that we are redeemed from the curse. Verse 14 tells us that the blessings of Abraham are ours. By faith, Abraham lived under the promise, not under the law. Every promise God made to Abraham is yours because you are not under the law of sin and death (Romans 8:2).

What's more, 2 Corinthians 1:20 (NIV) says, *"For no matter how many promises God has made, they are all yes in Christ."* This means that all the limitations of the Old Covenant promises are removed for those who are in Christ. Colossians 1:12 (NIV) says, *"...the Father...has qualified you to share in the inheritance of the saints in the kingdom of light."* Jesus has qualified you to receive all the promises, all of the inheritance of God.

"Faith comes by hearing, and hearing by the Word of God." Romans 10:17. A person is only able to operate faith based on the amount of the Word he has heard. Most Christians, even those who attend Full Gospel churches, have been taught to put unbiblical limitations on God: they haven't really "heard" the Full Gospel message. The church has taken the simple promises of God and made them complicated, putting conditions on them where none exist.

You see, God is waiting for us to make a decision. We must assume personal responsibility for what we believe. Until we make that decision, God has no room to work in our lives. The promises of God must be accepted without adding unbiblical stipulations.

Chapter 9

His Word Is Sufficient!

Why is it not enough for us to read the Bible and believe that what the Word says applies to us? We want God to speak to us personally, or maybe even audibly. How are we different from the children of Israel? We have trouble believing, just as they did, that God can cause us to triumph over insurmountable odds. Instead of mixing faith with the Word, we wait for God to speak to us individually. It may look like we are exercising faith when we do this, but what we are really doing is limiting God. In effect, we are saying that His written Word is not enough for us today — but His Word is sure (2 Peter 1:19). He is under no obligation to speak anything to us beyond what He has already said in the Bible.

In the Old Testament, God did not reveal His battle plans to *all* the Israelites; He revealed His plan only to the leaders. What would have happened if Israel had told Joshua, "We're not going to march around Jericho until we hear from God ourselves." No doubt, they would have ended up like the generation before them and died without entering the promised land. The armies of Israel acted on the Word of God in faith, and they won the battle. In the same way, we must act on the Word of God as written down for us in the Bible, whether or not we have any *special leading.*

Even if God gave you a special word, it would still require faith on your part to believe it and act on it. Paul told the Thessalonians that the reason the Word of God worked so effectively in their lives was because they did not receive it as the word of men, but *". . .as it is in truth, the Word of God that effectually worketh also in you that believe."* 1 Thessalonians 2:13.

What are we really saying when we refuse to believe the written Word of God? The Bible clearly states that Jesus died for all, and it is not the will of God that any should perish (2 Peter 3:9). But the promises of God are not automatic. People die and go to hell daily. God gave each of us a will of our own, and He does not violate our free will to force His will on us. When we refuse to accept the promises in the Bible as being true for us, we are limiting God. If the only way that God can fulfill the promises in our life is to violate our free will and force us to receive the promises, it will never happen!

Job 22:28 in the Amplified Bible says, *"You shall also decide and decree a thing, and it shall be established for you. . ."* God has told us His will. We must decide if we want His will in our lives. He says we must be *willing* to eat the good of the land. Many people want the good things of God but they are afraid to make a decision about it. If it is in God's Word, it is His will. If it is His will, we must decide to make it our will. We must boldly decree it in our lives. Then He will establish it.

Jesus said, *"Ask what you **will** when you pray."* John 15:7. We know what God's will is because the Bible tells us. We must set our will in agreement with God's will for our lives by believing what the Bible clearly tells us. If we do not do this, God will not violate our will to force us to receive the promises. If we do set our will in agreement with His by believing what the Bible says, then He has something He can bless.

The Word of God is absolute because the character of God is absolute and He changes not. The Bible says, *"No matter how many promises God ever made, they are yes in Jesus."* 2 Corinthians 1:20 (NIV). If you are in Jesus, then every promise in the Bible is for you.

In Matthew 8, a centurion came to Jesus on behalf of his servant who was ill. Jesus said, *"I will come and heal him."* The centurion had not placed any limitations on Jesus. His faith was not based on fulfilling some religious formula in order for healing to take place. He did not believe that healing could only occur if Jesus physically laid hands on the servant or if the servant physically got close enough to Jesus to touch the hem of His garment. He believed that Jesus had only to *say the Word* and his servant would be healed.

The Bible tells us that Jesus *marveled*. What was so amazing in the centurion's words that caused the Son of God to marvel? The children of Israel had the written Word of God, they had the covenant, and yet none of them understood faith and authority like this Roman centurion. The centurion had grasped the fact that the Word was enough! Everything else was form, ritual, superstition, or mere coincidence, which did not have a thing to do with whether or not a person got healed. Jesus was a Man of authority, and the centurion recognized and acknowledged His authority. His Word was sufficient.

His Word is *still* sufficient! To put conditions on what Jesus has told us is freely given, is to limit our own faith. And when we limit our faith, we limit the power of God in our lives.

Chapter 10

Commitment to Lordship

One of the main reasons there is such a lack of victory among Christians goes back to the way the Gospel was first presented to them. Most new Christians are taught to call upon Jesus for salvation, but they lack commitment to His Lordship because the concept of *Lordship* was not adequately explained to them.

Many people (and demons, too) know and believe that Jesus is the Son of God, but that knowledge alone is not sufficient for salvation. There must be a commitment to His Lordship. Nowhere in the New Testament is salvation promised apart from Lordship. The Bible does not teach us to call upon the

Name of the Savior, but rather to call upon the Name of the Lord. Salvation is what comes from making Jesus Lord.

There is even some confusion about just what it is we are to *confess with our mouth* when we get saved. Some people teach that we must confess our sins in order to be saved, but the Bible says we are to confess Jesus as Lord in order to be saved (Romans 10:9).

In the New Testament, the word *Lord* is used to mean an owner, master, or the one in control; in other words, *the boss*. If salvation is contingent upon making Jesus Lord, it is the obligation of the new convert to find the will of the Lord and do it. This process is not salvation by works: it is the fruit of repentance.

What is the salvation of the Lord? The word which is translated in the King James as *saved* is the Greek word: *sozo*. We have a tendency to limit our understanding of this word to the new birth. However, in Bible times, the word was clearly understood to involve much more than simply being born again.

Strong's Concordance defines *sozo* as "to deliver or protect: heal, preserve, save, do well, be whole." Thayer's Lexicon expands the definition to include: "to keep safe and sound, to rescue from danger or destruction, to make well, restore to health, to deliver from the penalties of Messianic judgment."

Let's look at how Jesus used the word *sozo*. In Matthew 1:21, the prophecy was given that Jesus would *sozo* the people from their sins. In Matthew 9, a woman with an issue of blood touched Jesus and was immediately healed. Jesus turned to her and said, *"Daughter, be of good comfort, thy faith has made thee **sozo**."* In Mark 6:56, multitudes of people were healed when they touched the hem of Jesus' garment. In the original language, it says, *"...as many as touched Him were made **SOZO**."*

We know that Jesus died to set us free from the results of sin so that we can partake in His salvation. We are *obligated* to receive every aspect of salvation. If Jesus is really our Lord, we do not have the option of refusing the abundant life. If Jesus is really our Lord, then we are under an obligation to reach the lost, to undo the works of the devil, to have the abundant life, and to do the things that He did (and greater!).

You must believe God will fulfill His promises. You must actively pursue those promises, not out of greed or even need, but because Jesus is Lord. You must allow His perfect salvation to be made manifest in your life. Salvation is more than a ticket to heaven. It is the sum total of what Jesus died to give us. It is the full, abundant life. Therefore, the abundant life should be the norm for every Christian. (It is the obligation, not the option, of every believer.)

Chapter 11

See God As He Is

The Bible says we reap what we sow (Galatians 6:7). One of the fruits of our sowing is the way we view God. We have a tendency to see God in the light of our own actions. For example, the less giving we do, the harder it is for us to see God as generous.

If we are to emerge from the negative thinking and unbelief in which we have been steeped, we must begin by seeing God as He really is. It is not enough to have a secondhand belief in God, no matter how sound the underlying doctrine. You must meet God for yourself through prayer and the Word.

As you read the Bible, mix it with prayer. Remember, you are not reading to find a list of "do's and don'ts," you are reading to have a personal encounter with God. You are getting to know a person, not a legal system. Read with your heart open, and pray with your Bible open. God will reveal Himself to you.

As you read, remind yourself of some basics. First of all, you are a New Covenant believer. Do not try to relate to God through *works righteousness*. It will always force you into legalism or self-righteousness. The only things from the Old Covenant that belongs to you are the promises. You are qualified to receive the promises because you are in Jesus.

You must have an absolute grasp of the fact that Jesus set you free from all the curses of the law. Galatians 3:13 tells us that Christ has redeemed us from the curse of the law by becoming a curse for us. We are delivered from the wrath of God (1 Thessalonians 5:9). God has reserved His judgment for the DAY of Judgment. Until that day comes, God is not judging anyone.

God loved you enough to send Jesus to die in your place. Do not treat the death of Jesus as a vain thing. Every sin that you ever committed was placed on Jesus. The Bible tells us that He became that sin (2 Corinthians 5:21). After taking our sin, He took the punishment our sins deserved. Every wrong thing you have ever done and every wrong thing you ever will do is covered by the Blood of Jesus. Jesus took the punishment so you would not have to take it.

God sent Jesus, through whom He would pour out His love on mankind. For God to judge you now and bring hardship into your life would be tantamount to rejecting the death of His Son. Romans 8:34 poses the question, *"Who is he that condemneth? . . . Christ that died . . ."* If Christ died for you, is He now going to condemn you? No! He did not come to condemn the world, but to save it.

God is a good God. James 1:16–17 says, *"Do not err, my beloved brethren. Every good and perfect gift is from above."* If this is true, why then, is God blamed for every bad thing that happens to mankind? When something bad befalls a sinner, much of the church world calls it God's judgment. If something bad befalls a righteous man, the same people call it God's sovereignty. James warned us not to make that error: God is a good God!

Remember, God is not a schizophrenic: He changes not (Malachi 3:6). He did not send His Son to set us free from the law of sin and death, only to change His mind and decide to put the curse of the law back on us again! It is the devil who brings sickness, poverty, and bondage, and then tries to get us to blame God for it!

Jesus said, *"The thief cometh not, but for to steal, and to kill, and to destroy: I am come that they might have life, and that they might have it more abundantly. I am the GOOD shepherd . . ."* John 10:10–11. This is the key to understanding the New Covenant. God does not do bad things to you, the devil does.

The most cunning thing the devil does is not to steal, kill, and destroy. Jesus told us he would do that. The most cunning thing the devil does is to steal, kill, and destroy, and *then convince us that God did it.* Satan brings the curse. Then he points out all your failures in order to convince you that God has sent you what you deserve.

All affliction and oppression is of the devil. Jesus came to free man from that oppression. In Luke 19:10, Jesus tells us that He came to seek and save that which was lost. First John 3:8 tells us that Jesus came to earth to destroy the works of the devil. Acts 10:38 tells us that Jesus went about doing good, and healing those who were oppressed of the devil. John 10:10 says He came to give us the abundant life. In John 14:12, Jesus said, *"He that believeth on Me, the works that I do, shall he do also; and greater works than these shall he do. . ."*

When Jesus sent His disciples forth to preach, He gave them a clear commission: *"And as ye go, preach, saying, the kingdom of heaven is at hand. Heal the sick, cleanse the lepers, raise the dead, cast out devils: freely ye have received, freely give."* Matthew 10:7–8. In John 20:21, Jesus tells us that we are sent, just as the Father sent Him. Our purpose and power on earth is the same as His: to undo the works of the devil. We are to take His Gospel and set people free from sin, poverty, sickness, and disease. We are to break the power of the devil over mankind. You see, Jesus has not changed His will for mankind. His ministry has not changed. Now, as then, His will is fulfilled through men who believe.

Jesus told His disciples in Matthew 10 that we are to *give* this Gospel in the same way that we receive it: *freely*. To give freely means more than without charge, Romans 3:24 says that we are justified freely by His grace. This means that we are justified by grace, apart from works. In the same way, we receive healing, miracles, and all the other promises of God by grace, not works. There are no conditions on what we are freely given, other than the need for faith.

"Why should God heal or prosper me?" you may ask, "I certainly don't deserve it." But Jesus did not instruct His disciples to heal only those who deserved it. He said, *"Freely you have received, freely give."* Matthew 10:8. Once we begin walking in love, and sharing the Gospel freely, we are then able to see God as One who freely gives. The only works God requires are the works that result from faith. According to James 2:20, *faith without works is dead.* Likewise, works without faith is dead.

When we believe God's promises, we act on that belief. We do not act expecting to earn the promises. Jesus did not put conditions on the people He healed. They did not earn their healing by good works. They got healed the same way you can — *freely.*

Chapter 12

God Is Love

More than anything else, God is love. When you enter the Holy of Holies, you find, not the Judgment Seat, but the Mercy Seat. When you get as deep in God as you can get, you find love as His eternal motivation.

First Corinthians 13 describes God's love: not the love that He requires of us alone, but the love that He demonstrated to us in the person of His Son. As you read this passage, insert the word *God* everywhere the word *love* appears. After all, God is love:

"God suffereth long, and is kind, God envieth not, God vaunteth not Himself, is not puffed up, does not behave Himself unseemly, seeketh not His own, is not easily provoked, thinketh no evil, rejoiceth not in iniquity, but rejoiceth in the truth. God beareth all things."

If God is love (and He is), we can now begin to understand Him and His goodness. When God commands us to walk in love, He exemplifies that same love towards us first. God is pouring blessings on you continuously. He wants you to receive them. He wants to show His goodness to you through the Lord Jesus.

God does not have a double standard. He gives the same love to us that He requires us to show to each other. First John 3:17 says, *"But whoso hath this world's good, and seeth his brother have a need, and shutteth up his bowels of compassion from him, how dwelleth the love of God in him?"* If God requires us to show compassion and generosity toward our brothers, will He not also do the same toward us? Matthew 7:11 says, *"If ye then, being evil, know how to give good gifts to your children, how much more shall your Father which is in heaven?"*

If you believe that God can heal you, but He won't because it is His will to keep you sick, how can you maintain a loving attitude toward Him? I find it hard to conceive how people can really love God as they ought if they believe that God treats His children that way.

I once found myself faced with a desperate financial need. I went to a friend who was more than able to help me through the crisis. He acknowledged that he had the means to help me, but for reasons of his own, he declined to do so. It was no small matter for me to overcome my bad attitude toward this friend who was able, but not willing, to help me in a time of legitimate need.

Blaming God for "unanswered" prayers becomes a *root of bitterness* for many Christians. In a time of need, they turned to God, but because they did not know how to operate the principles of faith, they were unable to receive from God and consequently, they felt that God was holding back on them.

Others say, "If God wants me to have it, He will give it to me." It *has* been given to you in the Lord Jesus, but you must do your part to claim it. Do not try to make God responsible for your lack!

How desperately we need to see that God has already given us *". . .all things that pertain unto life and godliness, through the knowledge of him that hath called us."* 2 Peter 1:3. God is not holding anything back from us. He has already given us **all things**. When Jesus died, He gave us everything we need, but it is by the knowledge of Him that we learn *how to lay hold of what we have been given.*

Several years ago, the Lord led me into a lengthy fast. During the last week of the fast, I checked into a hotel so I could be alone with God without distraction. I read every passage in the New Testament pertaining to love in every translation I owned. I began to see God in a totally different light. I saw love as the basis for all of His actions. During that week, God enabled me to truly enter into the love walk.

Since then, I have never wondered if it was God's will to meet any need that any person might have. Because He loves us so, He is always willing to meet our needs.

The apostle John said, *"We have known and believed the love that God hath to us."* 1 John 4:16. No matter how much someone loves you, it will be of no consequence if you do not know it and believe it. For the most part, mankind does not know and believe the love of God.

As you search the scriptures, ask the Holy Spirit to shed the love of God abroad in your heart. Ask for revelation knowledge about the love of God. Like the apostle John, we need to **know** and **believe** the love God has for us.

Until we become rooted and grounded in love, we tend to view faith merely as a means of obtaining something from God. But once we are able to see God's love for what it is, we can then see His provision as an expression of His love for us. It follows then that *failure to receive God's provision is really a rejection of the love of God.*

For years, I had desired great faith and power in my life. When I saw the love of God as it is, I realized that I had been seeking the wrong thing. *". . .To know the love of Christ, which passeth knowledge, that ye might be filled with all the fullness of God."* Ephesians 3:19. Once I knew and believed the love of God, faith and power appeared, too. The secret to having the fullness of God is to know the love of God.

Chapter 13

Establish a Biblical Sense of Self-Worth

Once you know who God is and how much He loves you, you can develop a Biblical sense of self-worth. This is an essential step in taking the limits off of God, because until you have a Biblical sense of self-worth, you may be able to see God's goodness for others, but you will not be able to see how it applies to you.

When you accepted Jesus, you became a new creation. The old passed away and all things became new (2 Corinthians 5:17). There is more to this newness than just being saved and starting over again. You now relate to God on an entirely different basis. When you are saved, you are *hid in Christ* (Colossians 3:3). In other words, when God looks at you, He sees Jesus. He relates to you as He relates to Jesus.

The word *repent* literally means to have a change of mind. When we get saved, we must read the Word, and through it, embark on the process of changing and renewing our minds in every area. We must continually seek the mind of Christ in His Word, and transform our thinking to mirror the written Word.

Many of us have difficulty accepting what God says about us. There are more than 130 scriptures in the New Testament that tells us who we are in Jesus. We are the righteousness of God in Christ (2 Corinthians 5:21). We are more than conquerors (Romans 8:37). We have victory over the world (1 John 5:5). Regardless of how it looks to you, this is how God sees it. It is your responsibility to renew your mind so that you can see it the same way God sees it.

The word *heresy* has its roots in a word which means to choose. As Christians, our views, opinions, and self-image need to line up with the Word of God. If we see something in the Word, but we choose to hold another view or opinion, that is heresy.

All that we are, all that we have, all that we do is because of who we are in Jesus. My self-worth comes from my identity in Christ. I no longer have to derive my self-worth from what I have struggled to accomplish. His accomplishments are mine. I am free from the pressure of works. I am free to receive this new identity by faith and walk in it by grace.

Colossians 1:12 says, *"The Father hath made us meet to be partakers of the inheritance of the saints in light."* The word *meet* means qualified. God has *qualified* us to receive all the inheritance, simply because we are in Jesus. We cannot boast of our works or our qualifications to receive from God. We can boast only in the work of the Lord Jesus Christ (Romans 3:27).

Once we realize that the work is accomplished in Jesus, we can worship and praise Him for what He has done. As we thank Him for our new identity, we are continually transformed into that likeness. As you worship Jesus and call Him your righteousness, you begin to have a heart of righteousness. As you acknowledge and confess your identity, the Holy Spirit will continue to give you revelation knowledge about your new identity.

Philemon 6 says, *"...the communication of thy faith may become effectual by the acknowledging of every good thing in you in Christ."* We must acknowledge before God the good things which are in us by Jesus. Another translation says it like this: *"We will have a full understanding of every good thing in us by Jesus."* I want to see myself as God sees me so I can walk in what He says I have.

Search the Bible for your identity scriptures and fill your heart with them. Never allow what other people say, or your own thoughts or past failures, cause you to see yourself in any way other than as God's Word describes you. *(You are what God says you are!)*

Chapter 14

Persuading Your Heart

The transformation in your thought life will not happen overnight. You did not get into the shape you are in overnight, either. It will take time and diligent effort for you to change the way you see yourself. You will be defying a lifetime of negative input. You will be resisting the negativity of the people around you. You will be confronting the religious world that would have you see yourself as "saved, but still a sinner."

The Bible says that Abraham was fully persuaded that God would do what He said He would do (Romans 4:21). Abraham was strong in faith, *giving glory to God.* He knew his body was as good as dead and the deadness of Sarah's womb. He also knew

God's promise to him did not depend on his circumstances or outward appearances. Therefore, he was able to praise and glorify God before the promise came to pass. As he worshipped God, he became stronger in his faith.

God dealt with Abraham for 25 years to get him to the place where he was immovable in his faith in the promises of God. You do not need to wait 25 years. Today, you have all the information you need about God's promises. Your heart must be persuaded that God's promises are true, and this revelation knowledge of the power of God will truly set you free.

You are born of the Spirit. He resides in you to teach you and lead you into truth. His job is to continually work to establish you in the grace of God. Your job is to fill your heart with the promises of God. Second Peter 1:4 says, *"Whereby are given unto us exceeding great and precious promises: that by these ye might be partakers of the divine nature, having escaped the corruption that is in the world through lust."*

Deuteronomy 6:6–9 gives us some understanding of what it means to have the Word in our heart: *"And these words, which I command thee this day, shall be in thine heart: And thou shalt teach them diligently unto thy children, and shalt talk of them when thou sittest in thine house, and when thou walkest by the way, and when thou liest down, and when thou risest up. And thou shalt bind them for a sign upon thine hand, and they shall be as frontlets between thine eyes. And thou shalt write them upon the posts of thy house, and on thy gates."*

So we are to talk about the Word with our family, put posters with scripture verses on our walls, wear jewelry with scripture verses engraved. In other words, any way you can find to hear, see, and say the Word of God. . .DO IT. Do it until your heart is full to overflowing with the promises of God.

Just as Pharaoh finally granted permission for Israel to leave Egypt, but then changed his mind and sent his armies in pursuit, likewise, you will find that your negative-thinking past will not let you go easily. The world wants you to stay defeated. The last thing Satan wants is another Christian who has taken the limits off of God!

Your heart has been filled with years of unbelief which must now be replaced. When you are ready to remove the limits from God in some area in your life, look up every scriptural promise that pertains to that area. Write them down. Confess them. Pray them. Discuss them with faith-filled friends and family. Purchase books and tapes that instruct you in that area. Do whatever it takes to get yourself in line with the Word of God.

We are saved by faith. Faith is believing and confessing God's promises. We must believe in our hearts what God says about Jesus. We must confess His Lordship with our mouths. Both are required in order for us to receive the promise of salvation. Faith is found in three places: first, in the Word; second, in our heart; third, in our mouth. If it is not found in all three places, it is not yet faith. Often we see something in the scripture, begin to confess it with our mouth, but never really believe it in our heart. That is not faith. A persuaded heart does not stagger under a load of unbelief (Romans 4:20).

"Take heed [to do] what you hear: with the measure you mete, it shall be measured unto you. . ." Mark 4:24. Just because you have read scripture, heard a sermon, or confessed a promise, does not

mean it will immediately come to pass in your life. The Word of God is not a magic formula.

Many of us have been taught to believe that confession itself *moves* God. But please understand that God has *already moved*. He sent Jesus, who translated us out of the kingdom of darkness and into the kingdom of light. Confession is not something we do to move God, it is something we do to persuade our hearts of what Jesus has already accomplished.

"How long will I have to do this reading, meditating, and confessing?" you ask. Simple, as long as it takes. The hungry eat until they are full. The thirsty drink until they are satisfied. You must read, meditate, pray, and confess until your heart is persuaded and the promises of God become life to you. Mark 4:24 in the Amplified Bible says it this way, ***"Be careful what you are hearing.*** *The measure [of thought and study] you give [to the truth you hear] will be the measure [of virtue and knowledge] that comes back to you, and more [besides] will be given to you who hear."*

If you really want to stop limiting God in some areas of your life, you will be able to do it in direct proportion to the degree of thought and study you give to His promises. By reading the Word, meditating on it, and confessing it, you bring your heart into line with what the Word says. As you meditate on God's promises in that area, they will become life to you — the transforming life of God. Do not give up on any promise until it is working in your life. It will happen when your heart is persuaded of the truth of God's Word.

We must recover our God-given ability to use our imaginations to see the unseen. We must read the Word of God and see our needs being met through His power, according to His promises. We must see ourselves healed, whole, and strong. We must see ourselves accomplishing all that God's Word says we can accomplish. We must persuade ourselves to remove all the unbiblical limitations we have placed on God. As we visualize the promises coming true in our own lives, we will persuade our hearts that God's Word is true.

Chapter 15

Operating Bold Faith

When your heart is persuaded, bold faith will develop naturally. You will no longer live in the realm of wondering and wavering. Regardless of the circumstances or the situation, your heart will be fixed in trust on the Lord.

The Bible says that faith without works is dead (James 2:20). It does not say that faith is missing; it says that without works, faith is in vain. I was taught that if I believed something in the Bible and it did not come to pass, it was because I did not believe enough. When I was making an effort to trust God more, I always wondered when I should act. I was waiting for some mystical timing of God. I know now that faith always produces some corresponding action.

When my faith became steadfast concerning God's will to heal in every situation, I knew immediately that I must carry this message to the world. I preached my first overseas crusade in a remote area of the world. As I preached on the promises of God to save, heal, and deliver, I must admit I quivered inwardly before the machete-toting natives.

The voice of unbelief (Satan) was telling me, "You don't feel the presence of God, and nothing is going to happen. You're going to give the invitation to pray for the sick, and no one will get healed. Not only will they reject God, but they will kill you, and cut you to pieces with their machetes." As I preached through the interpreter, I prayed inwardly, "God, it says in Your Word that You will heal the sick. I don't feel an anointing. I don't even feel Your presence, but I believe Your Word. I'm going to proclaim it boldly, and if it doesn't work, it's Your problem. I'm going to do my part. If they kill me, You can apologize to me when I get to heaven."

I continued to boldly proclaim God's promises. (I have found that boldness and confidence prompt faith in others.) When I gave the invitation to pray for the sick, I still felt nothing emotionally. Nevertheless, the first woman to come to the platform was healed of blindness and deafness. What followed was a flood of miracles. I had to put works with my faith, even when I felt nothing.

Another way to put works with your faith is through worship and thanksgiving. If you really believe a promise is for you, you should thank God for it as though you were already in possession of it. Praise Him for the truth of the promise.

James 2:22 says that faith is made perfect by works. If you want your faith to be perfect, start walking out the promise. You must defy any circumstance that opposes the Word of God. "But," you ask, "what happens if I do that, and I still don't see the results I need?" The Bible says we must let patience have her perfect work that we may be perfect and entire (James 1:4). Patience is the ability to stand under pressure without wavering.

Hebrews 10:35–36 says, *"Cast not away therefore your confidence, which hath great recompence of reward. For ye have need of patience, that, after ye have done the will of God, ye might receive the promise."* Many people operate real faith, but give up before receiving the promise. This is what is called vain faith. It is real, but it is in vain because it never bears fruit. Although they *do* believe, they do not continue in faith until the harvest comes in.

Remember, you are not waiting on God; you are bringing your heart into line with His Word. If you know the promise is yours, it is easier to hang in there for as long as it takes. It is not God's will for you to have to wait for the promise, but He will not violate your will. Once your heart lines up with the Word of God, you will truly believe and finally receive.

Several years ago, I made a quality decision. I determined that I would put nothing on my prayer list that I would not see through to the end. Since then, there have been many situations that have taken years to come to fruition. But God has never failed. If I do not quit, He always fulfills His promise.

I prayed for the salvation of an old friend of mine for eleven years. I witnessed to him whenever I got the chance, and I had many opportunities to become impatient or just give up on him. But whenever I thought of him, I just thanked God for the salvation that I was sure would come. A few years ago, I finally had the opportunity to lead him to the Lord.

Boldness is the by-product of faith. It is not an emotion. External boldness can be imitated, but real boldness is born of the confidence of knowing in your heart that the promise is yours, not merely wishing or hoping that it is.

Chapter 16

No More Limits

I am sure you have realized by now that taking the limits off of God is more than a formula. It is more than a method for obtaining the things we need or want. In fact, it is a scriptural mandate. It is time for us to quit making excuses for our unbelief and disobedience. It is time for us to start handling the precious promises of God with the absolute respect and honor that is due to His Word. It is time that we stop questioning and challenging the integrity of God. Any challenge of God's promises, regardless of the lofty theological language in which it is couched, is a challenge to the integrity of God. His name is only as good as His Word (Psalm 138:2).

When God created earth, He demonstrated His plan for man. He placed Him in a garden called paradise. All of man's needs were met. There was no sickness, no pain, no sorrow, no suffering. If those things had been the will of God for man, they would have existed in the garden. Adam lost that ideal life of God through the fall. But the fall did not change God's will for man.

With Israel, God once again demonstrated His will through a promise, by giving the children of Israel a PROMISED land. But because of their unbelief, they did not come into the fullness of what God wanted to give them: a land flowing with milk and honey, houses they did not build, gardens they did not plant, and victory over all their enemies.

The Jews had the opportunity to enter the promised land and show the world what God's intentions were toward mankind. Instead, they opted for a religious system that could not produce life. In the end, the entire world was turned off to God (Ezekiel 36:20). Likewise, the twentieth-century church has shown the world an empty religion instead of an almighty and all-loving God. When the world begins to see the God of the Bible, we will see the greatest revival ever witnessed on the face of the earth. All of man's efforts on the earth are an attempt to meet the needs that can only be met by his Creator.

In Jesus, we now have a promised land too—a dimension of life that will not only meet our needs, but will meet the needs of the world around us. Taking the limits off of God does not produce a selfish, greed-oriented lifestyle; it brings us into a dimension where we can feel the heart of God for the world. Once we are set free from the needs of this world through the promises of God (2 Peter 1:4), we are free to live for God instead of ourselves. When we truly experience the goodness and liberality of God, it becomes all but impossible to keep it to ourselves. We become compelled to see every human being experience this great love for themselves.

A life with no limits on God is a life with no room for fear, worry, or envy. It is a life of praise and devotion to the Lord Jesus Christ. To experience this great love and unlimited power working on our behalf is to fully understand what Jesus purchased in His death, burial, and resurrection.

In 1 John 3:2, we are told that we will become like Jesus when we see Him as He is. This revelation of an unlimited God brings with it the power to transform us into the likeness of the loving God we see. Jesus is calling us to enter in. He needs a church that will take all the unbiblical limits off God. Will you respond to His call? Will you enter in? Will you take the limits off God?

About the Author

James Richards is a pioneer in the field of faith-based human development. He has combined spirituality, energy medicine, scientific concepts and human intuition into a philosophical approach that brings about congruence in spirit, soul and body, resulting in incredible breakthroughs in health, emotional management, financial abundance and intimate connection with God. He is a life coach, consultant, teacher and motivational trainer. He holds doctorates in Theology, Alternative Medicine and Human Behavior. He was awarded an honorary doctorate in World Evangelism for years of service in the Philippines. His many certifications include: substance abuse counselor, detox specialist, herbalist, handwriting analysis, EFT, energy medicine and an impressive number of additional certifications and training certificates.

Dr. Richards has been successful as an entrepreneur who has built several successful businesses ranging from contracting to real estate to marketing. As a national best-selling author, Dr. Richards has written several books that have sold several million copies around the world. His most noted work is Heart Physics®, a life renewal program designed to equip people to transform any aspect of their life through changing the beliefs of their heart.

When asked why he has studied such a broad field his answer is simple: "If it helps people, I want to understand it!" The goal of all his work is to "help people experience wholeness: spirit, soul and body!"

To contact Dr. Richards, call or write:

Impact Ministries
3516 S. Broad Place
Huntsville, AL 35805

256-536-9402

256-536-4530 — Fax

www.impactministries.com

Other Publications by Dr. James B. Richards

Escape From Codependent Christianity

Grace: The Power to Change

Supernatural Ministry

The Gospel of Peace

The Prayer Organizer

Leadership That Builds People, Volumes 1 and 2

The Lost Art of Leadership

My Church, My Family: How to Have a Healthy
   Relationship with the Church

Becoming the Person You Want to Be: Discovering
   Your Dignity and Worth

Breaking the Cycle

How to Stop the Pain

We Still Kiss

Effective Small Group Ministry

Satan Unmasked: The Truth Behind the Lie

The Anatomy of a Miracle

Wired for Success, Programmed for Failure

Heart Physics®

**For more information on these and
Dr. Richards' other products, please visit:**

www.impactministries.com

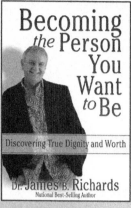